ITALIAN ALPHABET BOOK FOR CHILDREN

architettura · architecture

arte · art

A

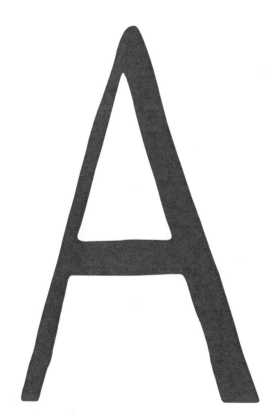

amore · love

Basilica di San Pietro · St. Peter's Basilica

B

bruschetta

grilled bread topped with
tomatoes, garlic, and olive oil

balcone · balcony

calciatore · footballer

caffè · coffee

C

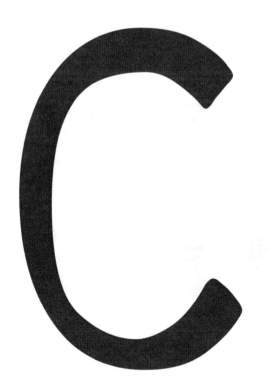

cucina · cuisine

D

dolce · sweet

doppio espresso · double espresso

esposizione · exhibition

estate · summer

F

formaggio · cheese

fiori · flowers

fiume · river

G

gondoliere · gondolier

gelato · ice cream

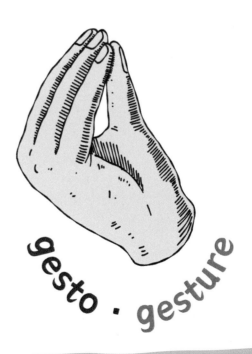

gesto · gesture

H

chiesa · church

spaghetti · spaghetti

chiacchiere · small talk

hamburger · hamburger

Italia · Italy

ingredienti · ingredients

L

lingua · language

latte · milk

lago · lake

M

moda · fashion

montagne · mountains

macchina · car

macinacaffè · coffee grinder

mamma · mother

mela · apple

mar Mediterraneo · Mediterranean Sea

N

nonna · grandmother

olive · olives

O

opera · opera

ospitalità · hospitality

P

pittura · painting

pasta · pasta

pomodoro · tomato

pane · bread

parmigiano · **parmesan**

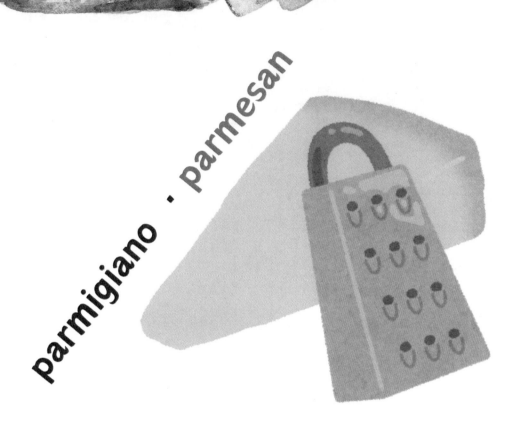

pizza · pizza

quercia · oak tree

R

Roma · Rome

ROME

ristorante · restaurant

ricetta · recipe

sole · sun

S

scultura · sculpture

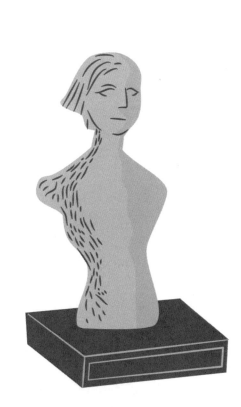

spiaggia · beach

La torre di Pisa · Leaning Tower of Pisa

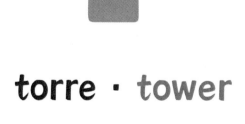

torre · tower

università · university

uva · grapes

uccello · bird

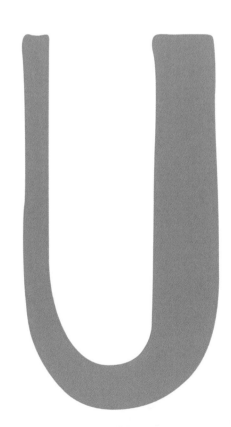

vino · wine

V

vulcano · vulcan

viaggio · journey

zucchero · sugar

zuppa · soup

zio · uncle

Z

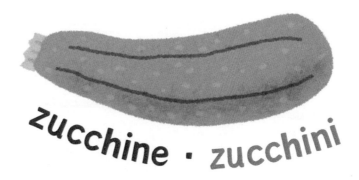

zucchine · zucchini

zucca · pumpkin

zia · aunt

Italian alphabet

A B C D E F G

H I L M N O P

Q R S T U V Z

Made in the USA
Las Vegas, NV
06 December 2024

13461391R20017